Winter Warmers

Silly & Serious

Poems to warm you through winter

Sandra Matthews

This book is dedicated to my Dad, John Ryan, who inspires me more than he will ever know.

My thanks to Ciaran for all his encouragement. Also, thanks to April, Evan and Amaya for their help in content editing, layout and font.

Note from the author:

Thank you so much for reading my first book of poems. I hope they speak to you.

I've been writing for years, but this is my first time to publish anything, which is exciting and a bit scary. Mostly though, I'm just glad to finally do it.

I hope you are also reaching for things that scare and excite you.

And on with the writing I go.

Love Sandra

https:/www.matthews-sandra.com

www.facebook.com/sandramatthewsireland.com/

Contents

POETRY IS

Poetry is odd
Author thinks they're God
Vomiting up words
To tickle a reader's ear
Can't see yourself reading
Sipping your favourite beer

OR

Poetry is hip
Takes us on a trip
Puts into words
The ups and downs we feel
Young and old are reading
Words can touch and heal

FIRELIGHT

Loneliness stung sharpest at the weekend
Kids do their own thing
No longer hide in mother's wing

Firelight is the bright spark of company
That sat and warmed me
Through that hollow time
Never rushed away
Or cancelled on the day
Its attention ever fully mine

Loneliness no longer calls so often
Sweeter now is life
Flavoured with ordinary strife

Firelight is still a cherished visitor
Sits and warms me
Happy here to dwell
Asks that I feed it
There when I need it
Warms my soul to see its sparkling spell

STARVE

Food gives us heat
Without it we'd be cold

And though they say we need less
As we gracefully grow old

The experts here are wrong
They cannot be right

I'm still prone to hunger
On a cold winter night

And though my jeans are tight
I must keep myself fuelled

To starve a person of my age
Seems a step too cruel

FART

Squeeze tight
You can do it
Hold
Until it passes

As you grip
Keep praying
That this
Motley stew of gasses

Is the sweetest kind
In silence leaks from one's behind

Then no one else need
Ever know nor mind

Unless you were to write
A poem confessing
In that case you're a lost cause
Too dumb to keep 'em guessing

PLEASE MAM

Please Mam
Please
Pretty please
My keys are in the house

I rushed out this morning
So I would not miss the bus
I don't know what to do
I'm stressed out by this fuss

Please Mam
Please
Pretty please
I need my keys right now

I thought you'd be at home
So that you could let me in
I don't know what to do
I simply cannot win

Please Mam
Please
Pretty please
I'll bring my keys next time
I need you to come home
So I can change my bags
I don't know what to do
I can't go in these rags

Please Mam
Please
Pretty please
Your friends will understand
Sure aren't you always saying
We should lend a helping hand

YEARNING

October evenings fall
Into November ways
December chases close behind
Eager for our praise

With logs in leaping firelight
Clean sprinkling falls of snow
Hot chocolate with marshmallows
Warm house where windows glow

Yes, yes, I hear you
Such comforts light our way
Yet no, the yearning does not stop
For spring with brighter day

GOOD BYE

She'll be there to spend the winter
And many winters more
Has sold her house
Packed her bags
For life on Canada's shores

Friendship is a wonder
A joy
A pain
A leap
We let ourselves be open
Yet friends
Can
Never
Keep
A reign on freedom's call

I'm just home from the airport run
Time alone to let tears cry
She has been my friend
Just three years
But it's still hard to say goodbye

CHRISTMAS IN DECEMBER

October is in autumn
Please give it its day
To trick and treat on local streets
Chase falling leaves with cooling feet
Lost in the season's trance

November starts the winter
Please give it a chance
To have its own rich part to play
Before it must give right of way
To the Christmas dance

December starts the countdown
Please do let us wait
To plan and prep and party much
With family, friends, work and church
Join the Yuletide prance

CLAUSTROPHOBIC DARKNESS

Claustrophobic darkness
Rising
Haughtily
Higher

Persistent in desire

Climbs over minutes
Pursuing sweet hours

Relentlessly
Our precious daylight
Devours

COLD

Cold creeps in uninvited
Goes first for hands and feet
Climbs up onto the bed
Soaks deep into your sheet

Grabs hold of your nose
Tight it clamps to freeze
Hunts for limbs uncovered
Shoots chills up legs and sleeves

Cold has no manners
Cares not how we feel
Wrap up in many layers
Fight back with heated zeal

MORNING WALK

Cold morning walk
Scarf wrapped tight
Dog sniffs and searches
No one else in sight

Alone with my dog
He knows scandals deep
Woman's trusted confidante
Will all my secrets keep

Sting of sharp breeze
Hat pulled down
Peace of quiet stroll
In sleepy local town

Lights switching on
Breakfast time is near
Deliciousness of silence
My favourite sound to hear

CANCELLED PLANS

Joy of cancelled plans
Night by crackling fire
Change into pyjamas
Pull the blanket higher

Dust off that novel
Too long on the shelf
Wallow in the free
Time to myself

Or turn on TV show
Watch by fire's glow
Smug to simply know
I can let the evening flow

Or get an early night
Warm in duvet fleece
Either way I'm breathing in
A sigh of deep relief

I did not cancel
This is not on me
Another person takes the wrap
I am guilt free

MAM'S DOWNSTAIRS

Mam sits on the couch
Turns on her favourite show
Message spreads
Fast and wide
"Mam's downstairs, go, go, go"

Race to join her there
Pause that silly show
Share your cares
Deep and true
Mam will listen, we all know

Mam may look well rested
Sitting there alone
But she needs
Us to save her
From this mindless TV zone

GUILTY

Time to read a book
Or watch morning TV
Feel a little guilty
As if I should not be

Sitting on my bum
While around me
There is mess

Never ending laundry
And the hem
On my daughter's dress

Needs to be mended
If I can remember how
Sewing is a task that
Brings sweat beads to my brow

Time to cook the dinner
Serve up menu suave
Feel a little guilty
As if I should not have

Sat and read that book
Or watched that silly show
Now it's almost six
And my progress is too slow

Need to be speeding
If I can remember how
Cooking is a task that
Brings furrows to my brow

Now I pause to sit
And take the pressure off
Dinner won't be ready
And I'm feeling hot and cross

My own fault for reading
And watching some TV
Soon loved ones will be home
And the mess still clear to see

DECEMBER TWENTY-FIRST

We pass December twenty-first
Minute by minute days grow
Shadows of winter pride
Numbered
Though darkness still seems
In full flow

Then bitter days' fall
My hope can see
Spring is naughtily
Waving at me

Let us count down
The minutes together
Winter though cruel
Will not last forever

WINTER FUNERAL

By graveside
Raw cold winter day
Sending a loved one on their way

Tears of goodbye
Freezing to our face
Desolate is this wretched place

Season of death
Nature falls apart
Echoing pangs of broken hearts

I TURNED AROUND

I turned around
That's all
No leap or fall or careless climb

Stuck
Right
There
Beside
Checkout
Counter

Nothing would help
At all
Spasm would pass in its own good time

Kids
Were
Wishing
The
Ground
Would
Open

OUCHY

Ow, that hurts
Ooh, I'm stiff
Slow down and wait for me

Hobbling for a moment
Until I get my stride
Trying hard to keep up
When walking by her side

Standing up from sitting long
My friends and I now sing a song
Of achey here and ouchy there
Appointments with physios
We compare

Youth may make more noise
As their music blares around
We just stand up from the couch
And make old people sounds

Ooh ow aaah
Need to slowly stand
Please lend me your hand

PACKAGE

Sent my parcel
To a certain motel
Best not say the name
Lest it rings alarm bell

Received a message
From said motel
Best go collect
Thinking all would be well

I stood like an eejit
For half an hour
Excitements turning
To feeling sour
This silly machine
With buttons galore
Had me pressing so much
My fingers were sore

I called the office
And made a complaint
My tone neither rude
Nor as sweet as a saint

They listened but
Could not understand
Why a simple process
Had got out of hand

Then like a bolt horror struck
What a horrible holy muck
Up I had made
Wasting my day
Having my say
Complaining away

When just up the road
Was my precious load
Exactly where it was meant to be
If I had opened my eyes to see

Hanging my head
In embarrassed shame
I prayed they would
Never remember my name

ELEVEN YEARS

Mam is gone eleven years
It no longer hurts so much
Still Christmas brings refreshing
To the memory of her touch
Her voice, her smile, her giggle
We were a giddy pair
Finding humour often
In the midst of aching care

Mam is gone eleven years
Yet I could not
Write this
Without tears
And Christmas stirs
This pain of mine
Even when
I think I'm fine

Let us mind each other
When celebrations
Make us sad
With feelings sentimental
For the times we might have had

FANCY STEWS

One pot wonders make my day
(Fancy stews, one might say)

How fabulous it feels
To have dinner organised
A simple thing like this
Is cause for joy and pride

Not for me the hassle
Of many pots and pans
Chuffed to have a dinner
That I actually planned

Tomorrow I may be
In pure chaotic mess
Today I shine my halo
Domestic Goddess

PONDER THAT

Christmas is what you make it
Mam would always say
Back in the day
I had yet seen nothing
Of the misery it can bring
For they who every year
Must stand alone to sing
Their festive songs
Or sleep on icy footpaths
December 24th
As on every other night
Their bed is made
Of concrete disappointments
As we prepare for lovely surprises

Christmas is what you make it
Let us ponder that

WRONG SIZE

T'was Christmas Eve
When I realised
The trousers for my hubby
Were in the wrong size

I should have just told him
He would have understood
But no, I took the high way
To be the wifey good

Off I went for shopping
On the craziest of days
Somehow I did manage
To park and find my way

Got the size I wanted
Queued with aching back
Never again will I join in
The Christmas Eve attack

SANTA

Santa no longer stops for me
I'm really very old
His gifts are for the children
Who try to sleep
With eyes shut tight
Wondering what presents
He will bring them tonight

Santa no longer stops for me
I'm really very old
His reindeer cross the night sky
They try to land
On houses bright
Wondering which chimneys
Will be wide or tight

Santa can manage anyhow
The reindeer simply worry
For every Christmas Eve
It seems they are in a hurry

RELATIVES ARE COMING

The relatives are coming around
Help from the kids cannot be found

They tell me to relax
Why must the house be clean
No one else will notice
Sure I'm just a drama queen

The bathroom is disastrous
They ask me who will care
I for one am freaked out
Don't want a judging stare

Not that anyone would say much
But I'd know what they'd be thinking:
What's happened to our sis
Her standards are surely sinking

So on I go with the cleaning
I'll have the place soon gleaming
My kids would not be rude
They will help to eat the food

MUCKY FLOORS

Never ending muck is a gift that keeps on giving
Reminding us to cherish the sweet climate we live in

Drought a rarity
Except in summer hot
No luscious grass in Spain
They do not enjoy our rain
Taste of golden butter makes it worth the pain

These thoughts we keep in mind
As we count paw prints on the floor
Leading to the front
From the back door
Not even a suggestion That we might think to roar
Or threaten that we cannot
Mop this any more

Our character is such
We'd not complain too much
Instead we call it lucky
To live with floors so mucky

DAYS AFTER CHRISTMAS

These days after Christmas
Throw dark clouds our way
Celebrations done
We are left with bills to pay

Facing into starkness
Of how much money spent
Celebrations over
We are left to pay the rent

Summer's silly days
Seem far out of sight
Celebrations past
We are left to frugal nights

Will we ever learn
To consider our future selves
Or always will we fall
For deals on shops' bright shelves

NEW YEAR NEW YOU

Don't get me started
This is a pet hate
Something you hear
So much of late

New Year New You
Was the old you wrong
No longer skinny enough
To wear, well, a thong

Did the old you run marathons
The new you certainly must
And while you are doing that
Set up a trust
Or a business
Or write a big book
All the while working hard
On your new look

Whatever you do
Send the old you away
Only new versions
Are welcome to play

STRESS NOT

Teeny tiny changes
Are the only kind
I have any chance
With at all

Take on alterations big
And surely
Soon I am guaranteed to fall

I've tried and tried and tried in desperation
No longer waste my time in false anticipation

Perhaps there is a tiny thing
That you might change
By this time next year
How it might have sprouted

Small changes give us back
Our hope of freedom
At least it's worth a try
I do not doubt it

MOST EMBARRASSING FART

T'was a cold winter's evening
When we gathered for dinner
Warm comforting chilli
Always a winner

We then dispersed to various rooms
For study, TV or meetings on zoom

When I noticed it brewing
Hoped t'would easily pass
Discreet in the manner
Of ladylike gas

Accepted I then
This was not the case
Aimed but to hide
Panicked look from my face

Sought out the most remote
Part of the house
Safely away from
Offspring or spouse
Quickly I hurried there
Cheeks squeezing tight
Closed door and set free
Its thundering might

Sighed in relief
To have found a safe zone
Switched light on to find
I was not alone

He'd been silent in dark
And meditative space
Now he wore shock, horror
Over his face

SERIES & MORE

This book is part of a series called

Silly & Serious Seasonal Poetry

Watch out for them as they are released over the coming year.

Another book also coming soon will include most of my favourites written over the last ten years or more. Some of them have been used in my Facebook Poetry Videos.

Thanks again for reading.

If you like these poems I would so appreciate your review (hopefully good) on Amazon.

Love Sandra

https:/www.matthews-sandra.com

www.facebook.com/sandramatthewsireland.com/

Printed in Great Britain
by Amazon

32809277R00026